Christmas Carols
23 classic carols for keyboard

Published 1996

Series Editor Anna Joyce
Design & Art Direction Dominic Brookman

Music arranged & processed by Barnes Music Engraving Ltd East Sussex TN34 1HA
Cover Image © Adam Wolfitt/Corbis

© International Music Publications Ltd
Griffin House 161 Hammersmith Road London England W6 8BS

Angels, From The Realms Of Glory

Words by James Montgomery / Music French traditional

Suggested Registration: Glockenspiel
Rhythm: Soft Rock
Tempo: ♩ = 112

An-gels, from the_ realms of glo-ry, wing your flight o'er_ all the earth;

Ye who sang Cre - a - tion's sto - ry now pro - claim Mes - si - ah's birth!

Come _____ and__

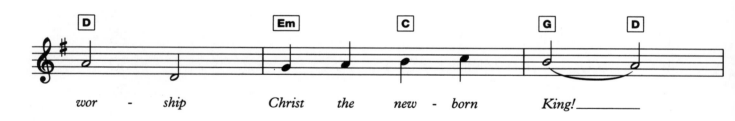

wor - ship Christ the new - born King! _____

Come _____ and__

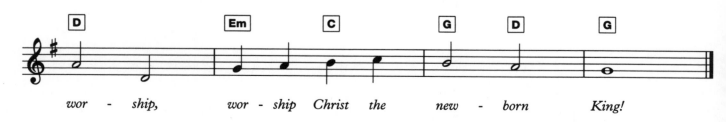

wor - ship, wor - ship Christ the new - born King!

1   Angels, from the realms of glory,
      Wing your flight o'er all the earth;
      Ye who sang Creation's story
      Now proclaim Messiah's birth!
        Come and worship Christ the new-born King!

2   Shepherds, in the field abiding,
      Watching o'er your flocks by night:
      God with man is now residing,
      Yonder shines the Infant Light.
        Come and worship . . .

3   Sages, leave your contemplations:
      Brighter visions beam afar.
      Seek the Great Desire of Nations:
      Ye have seen his natal star.
        Come and worship . . .

4   Saints, before the altar bending,
      Watching long in hope and fear:
      Suddenly the Lord, descending,
      In his temple shall appear.
        Come and worship . . .

5   Though an infant now we view him,
      He shall fill his Father's throne,
      Gather all the nations to him;
      Every knee shall then bow down.
        Come and worship . . .

Am 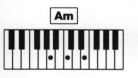 **C** 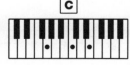 **D**  **E7**  **Em**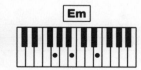

G

Away In A Manger

Words traditional / Music by William J Kirkpatrick

Suggested Registration: Strings
Rhythm: Waltz
Tempo: ♩ = 88

A - way in a____ man - ger, no____

crib for a bed, the___ lit - tle Lord Je - sus laid___

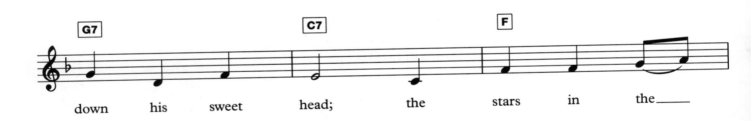

down his sweet head; the stars in the____

bright sky looked__ down where he lay, the___

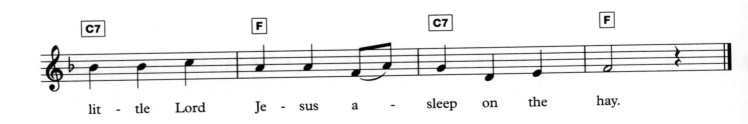

lit - tle Lord Je - sus a - sleep on the hay.

1   Away in a manger,
    No crib for a bed,
    The little Lord Jesus
    Laid down his sweet head;
    The stars in the bright sky
    Looked down where he lay,
    The little Lord Jesus
    Asleep on the hay.

2   The cattle are lowing,
    The baby awakes,
    But little Lord Jesus,
    No crying he makes.
    I love thee, Lord Jesus!
    Look down from the sky,
    And stay by my side
    Until morning is nigh.

3   Be near me, Lord Jesus,
    I ask thee to stay
    Close by me for ever,
    And love me, I pray;
    Bless all the dear children
    In thy tender care,
    And bring us to heaven,
    To live with thee there.

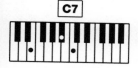
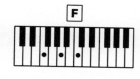
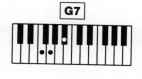
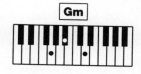

CHRISTIANS AWAKE

Words by John Byrom / Music by John Wainwright

Suggested Registration: French Horn
Rhythm: March
Tempo: ♩ = 120

1 Christians awake, salute the happy morn,
Whereon the Saviour of the world was born!
Rise to adore the mystery of love,
Which hosts of angels chanted from above;
With them the joyful tidings first begun
Of God incarnate and the Virgin's Son.

2 Unto the watchful shepherds it was told,
Who heard the angelic herald's voice: 'Behold!
I bring good tidings of a Saviour's birth
To you and all the nations of the earth:
This day hath God fulfilled his promised word,
This day is born a Saviour, Christ the Lord!'

3 'In David's city, shepherds, ye shall find
The long-foretold Redeemer of mankind;
Joseph and Mary, in a stable there,
Guard the sole object of the Almighty's care;
Wrapped up in swaddling-clothes, the Babe divine
Lies in a manger: this shall be your sign.'

4 He spake, and straightway the celestial choir
In hymns of joy, unknown before, conspire.
The praises of redeeming love they sung,
And heaven's whole orb with hallelujahs rung;
God's highest glory was their anthem still,
Peace on the earth, and mutual good will.

5 To Bethlehem straight the enlightened shepherds ran
To see the wonder God had wrought for man,
And found, with Joseph and the blessèd Maid,
Her Son, the Saviour, in a manger laid:
To human eyes none present but they two,
Where heaven was pointing its concentred view.

6 Amazed, the wondrous story they proclaim,
The first apostles of his infant fame;
While Mary keeps and ponders in her heart
The heavenly vision which the swains impart,
They to their flocks, still praising God, return,
And their glad hearts within their bosoms burn.

7 Let us, like these good shepherds, then, employ
Our grateful voices to proclaim the joy;
Like Mary, let us ponder in our mind
God's wondrous love in saving lost mankind:
Artless and watchful as these favoured swains,
While virgin meekness in our heart remains.

8 Trace we the Babe, who has retrieved our loss,
From his poor manger to his bitter Cross,
Treading his steps, assisted by his grace,
Till man's first heavenly state again takes place,
And, in fulfilment of the Father's will,
The place of Satan's fallen host we fill.

9 Then may we hope, the angelic thrones among,
To sing, redeemed, a glad triumphal song.
He that was born upon this joyful day
Around us his glory shall display;
Saved by his love, incessant we shall sing
Of angels, and of angel-men the King.

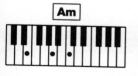
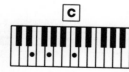

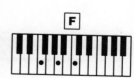
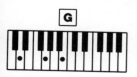

DECK THE HALL WITH BOUGHS OF HOLLY

Welsh traditional

Suggested Registration: Piano
Rhythm: Country Rock
Tempo: ♩ = 80

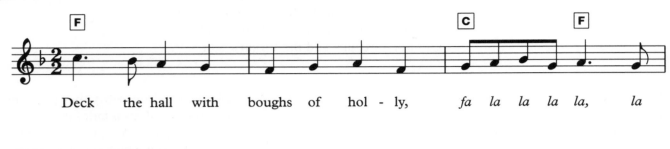

Deck the hall with boughs of hol - ly, *fa la la la la, la*

la la la. 'Tis the sea - son to be jol - ly,

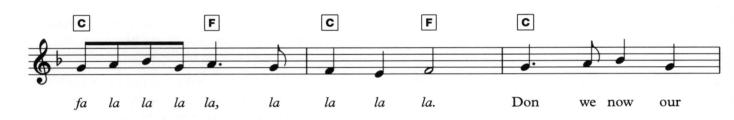

fa la la la la, la la la la. Don we now our

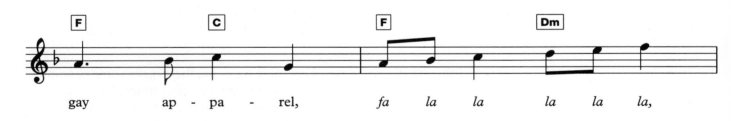

gay ap - pa - rel, *fa la la la la la,*

la la la. Troll the an - cient yule - tide ca - rol,

fa la la la la, la la la la.

1 Deck the hall with boughs of holly,
Fa la la la la, la la la la.
'Tis the season to be jolly,
Fa la la la la, la la la la.
Don we now our gay apparel,
Fa la la, la la la, la la la.
Troll the ancient yuletide carol,
Fa la la la la, la la la la.

2 See the blazing yule before us,
Fa la la la la, la la la la.
Strike the harp and join the chorus,
Fa la la la la, la la la la.
Follow me in merry measure,
Fa la la, la la la, la la la.
While I tell of yuletide treasure,
Fa la la la la, la la la la.

3 Far away the old year passes,
Fa la la la la, la la la la.
Hail the new, ye lads and lasses,
Fa la la la la, la la la la.
Sing we joyous all together,
Fa la la, la la la, la la la.
Heedless of the wind and weather,
Fa la la la la, la la la la.

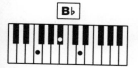
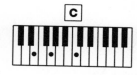
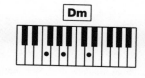
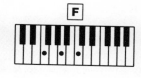

Ding! Dong! Merrily On High

Words by Woodward and Wood / Music by Thoinot Arbeau

Suggested Registration: Clarinet
Rhythm: Country Rock
Tempo: ♩ = 80

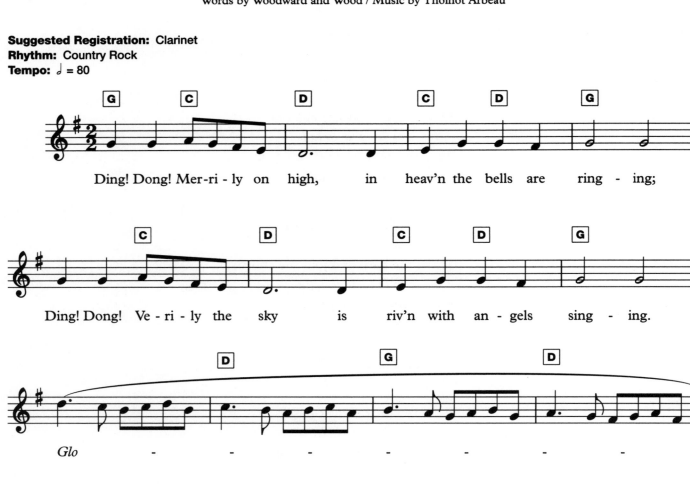

Ding! Dong! Mer-ri-ly on high, in heav'n the bells are ring-ing;

Ding! Dong! Ve-ri-ly the sky is riv'n with an-gels sing-ing.

Glo - - - - - - - -

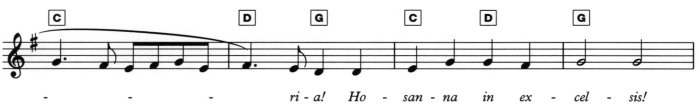

- - - ri-a! Ho-san-na in ex-cel-sis!

Glo - - - - - - -

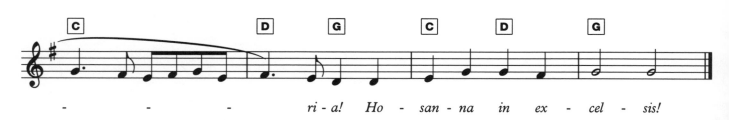

- - - ri-a! Ho-san-na in ex-cel-sis!

1   Ding! Dong! Merrily on high,
       In heav'n the bells are ringing;
       Ding! Dong! Verily the sky
       Is riv'n with angels singing.
          Gloria! Hosanna in excelsis!

2   E'en so here below, below,
       Let steeple bells be swungen,
       And 'Io, io, io!'
       By priest and people sungen.
          Gloria . . .

3   Pray you, dutifully prime
       Your matin chime, ye ringers!
       May you beautifully rime
       Your evetime song, ye singers!
          Gloria . . .

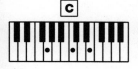
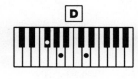
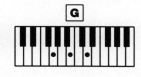

The First Nowell

Traditional

Suggested Registration: French Horn
Rhythm: Waltz
Tempo: ♩ = 112

1 The first Nowell the angel did say,
 Was to certain poor shepherds in fields as they lay.
 In fields where they lay keeping their sheep,
 On a cold winter's night that was so deep.
  Nowell, Nowell, Nowell, Nowell,
  Born is the King of Israel.

2 They lookèd up and saw a star,
 Shining in the east, beyond them far,
 And to the earth it gave great light,
 And so it continued both day and night.
  Nowell . . .

3 And by the light of that same star,
 Three wise men came from country far;
 To seek for a king was their intent,
 To follow the star wherever it went.
  Nowell . . .

4 This star drew nigh to the north-west,
 O'er Bethlehem it took its rest,
 And there it did both stop and stay
 Right over the place where Jesus lay.
  Nowell . . .

5 Then entered in these wise men three
 Full reverently upon their knee,
 And offered there in his presence
 Their gold, and myrrh, and frankinsense.
  Nowell . . .

6 Then let us all with one accord,
 Sing praises to the heavenly Lord,
 That hath made heaven and earth of nought
 And with his blood mankind hath bought.
  Nowell . . .

C

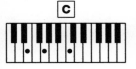

F

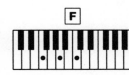

G

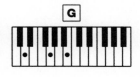

GOD REST YOU MERRY, GENTLEMEN

Traditional

Suggested Registration: Trumpet
Rhythm: Soft Rock
Tempo: ♩ = 84

God rest you mer - ry, gen - tle - men! Let no-thing you dis-

-may. Re - mem - ber Christ our Sa - viour was born on Christ-mas

Day, to save us all from Sa - tan's power when

we had gone a - stray. Oh,_____ tid - ings of

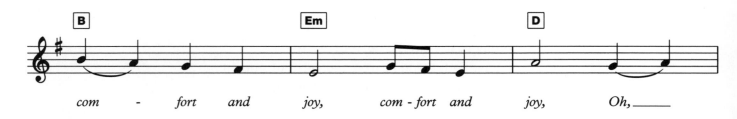

com - fort and joy, com - fort and joy, Oh,_____

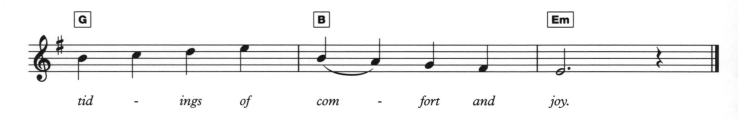

tid - ings of com - fort and joy.

1 God rest you merry, gentlemen!
   Let nothing you dismay.
   Remember Christ our Saviour
   Was born on Christmas Day,
   To save us all from Satan's power
   When we had gone astray.
   Oh, tidings of comfort and joy,
   Comfort and joy,
   Oh, tidings of comfort and joy.

2 In Bethlehem, in Jewry,
   This blessèd Babe was born,
   And laid within a manger,
   Upon this blessèd morn;
   To which his mother Mary
   Did nothing take in scorn.
   Oh, tidings . . .

3 From God our heavenly Father,
   A blessèd angel came;
   And unto certain shepherds
   Brought tidings of the same:
   How that in Bethlehem was born,
   The Son of God by name.
   Oh, tidings . . .

4 'Fear not then,' said the angel,
   'Let nothing you affright,
   This day is born a Saviour
   Of a pure Virgin bright,
   To free all those who trust in him
   From Satan's power and might.'
   Oh, tidings . . .

5 The shepherds at those tidings,
   Rejoicèd much in mind,
   And left their flocks a-feeding,
   In tempest, storm and wind:
   And went to Bethlehem straightway,
   The Son of God to find.
   Oh, tidings . . .

6 And when they came to Bethlehem,
   Where our dear Saviour lay,
   They found him in a manger,
   Where oxen feed on hay;
   His blessèd mother, Mary
   Unto the Lord did pray.
   Oh, tidings . . .

7 Now to the Lord sing praises,
   All you within this place,
   And with true love and brotherhood,
   Each other now embrace;
   This holy tide of Christmas,
   All other doth efface.
   Oh, tidings . . .

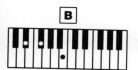
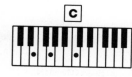
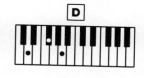
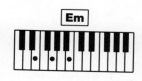
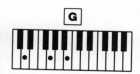

Good Christian Men, Rejoice

Traditional

Suggested Registration: Accordian
Rhythm: Shuffle
Tempo: ♩. = 88

Good Christ - ian men, re - joice, _____ with

heart and soul and voice. _____ Give ye heed to

what we say: News! News! Je - sus Christ is

born to - day. Ox and ass be - fore him bow, and

he is in a man - ger now, Christ is born to -

- day! _____ Christ is born to - day! _____

1   Good Christian men, rejoice,
    With heart and soul and voice.
    Give ye heed to what we say:
        News! News!
    Jesus Christ is born today.
    Ox and ass before him bow,
    And he is in a manger now,
        Christ is born today!
        Christ is born today!

2   Good Christian men, rejoice,
    With heart and soul and voice.
    Now ye hear of endless bliss:
        Joy! Joy!
    Jesus Christ was born for this:
    He hath oped the heavenly door,
    And man is blessèd evermore.
        Christ was born for this:
        Christ was born for this.

3   Good Christian men, rejoice,
    With heart and soul and voice.
    Now ye need not fear the grave:
        Peace! Peace!
    Jesus Christ was born to save!
    Calls you one and calls you all,
    To gain his everlasting hall:
        Christ was born to save!
        Christ was born to save!

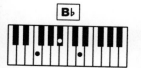
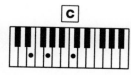
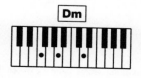
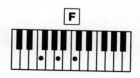

Good King Wenceslas

Words by J M Neale / Music traditional

Suggested Registration: Clarinet
Rhythm: Swing
Tempo: ♩ = 152

Good King Wen - ces - las looked out on the feast of Ste - phen,

when the snow lay round a - bout, deep and crisp and

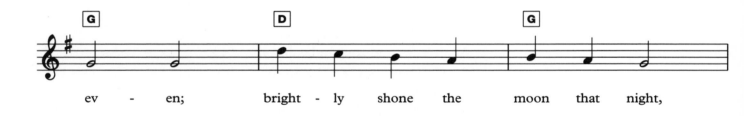

ev - en; bright - ly shone the moon that night,

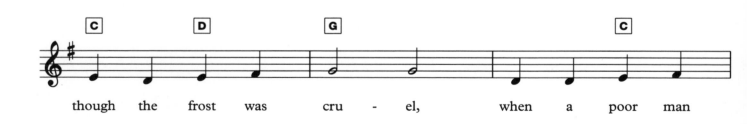

though the frost was cru - el, when a poor man

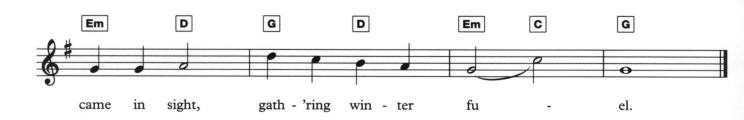

came in sight, gath - 'ring win - ter fu - el.

1   Good King Wenceslas looked out
    On the feast of Stephen,
    When the snow lay round about,
    Deep and crisp and even;
    Brightly shone the moon that night,
    Though the frost was cruel,
    When a poor man came in sight,
    Gath'ring winter fuel.

2   'Hither, page, and stand by me,
    If thou know'st it, telling –
    Yonder peasant, who is he?
    Where and what his dwelling?'
    'Sire, he lives a good league hence,
    Underneath the mountain;
    Right against the forest fence,
    By St Agnes' fountain.'

3   'Bring me flesh, and bring me wine,
    Bring me pine-logs hither;
    Thou and I will see him dine,
    When we bear them thither.'
    Page and monarch forth they went,
    Forth they went together,
    Through the rude wind's wild lament,
    And the bitter weather.

4   'Sire, the night is darker now,
    And the wind blows stronger;
    Fails my heart, I know not how,
    I can go no longer.'
    'Mark my footsteps, good my page,
    Tread thou in them boldly;
    Thou shalt find the winter's rage
    Freeze thy blood less coldly.'

5   In his master's steps he trod,
    Where the snow lay dinted:
    Heat was in the very sod
    Which the saint has printed.
    Therefore, Christian men, be sure –
    Wealth or rank possessing –
    Ye who now will bless the poor,
    Shall yourselves find blessing.

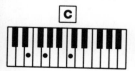
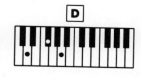
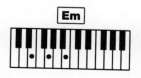
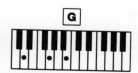

Hark! The Herald Angels Sing

Words by Charles Wesley and others / Music by Felix Mendelssohn

Suggested Registration: Church Organ
Rhythm: Soft Rock
Tempo: ♩ = 112

Hark! The her - ald an - gels sing, 'Glo - ry to the
new - born King! Peace on earth and mer - cy mild,

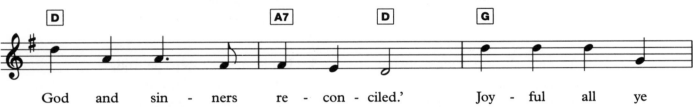

God and sin - ners re - con - ciled.' Joy - ful all ye

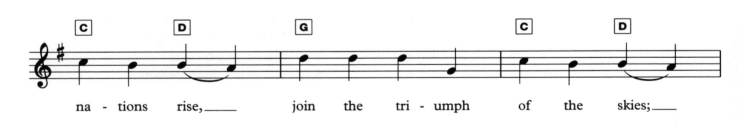

na - tions rise, join the tri - umph of the skies;

With th'an - gel - ic hosts pro - claim, 'Christ is born in Beth - le - hem!'

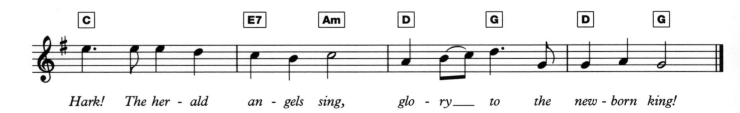

Hark! The her - ald an - gels sing, glo - ry to the new - born king!

1   Hark! The herald angels sing,
     'Glory to the new-born King!
     Peace on earth and mercy mild,
     God and sinners reconciled.'
     Joyful all ye nations rise,
     Join the triumph of the skies;
     With th'angelic hosts proclaim,
     'Christ is born in Bethlehem!'
       Hark! The herald angels sing,
       Glory to the new-born king!

2   Christ, by highest heaven adored,
     Christ, the everlasting Lord,
     Late in time behold him come,
     Offspring of a Virgin's womb.
     Veiled in flesh the Godhead see!
     Hail th'incarnate Deity!
     Pleased as man with man to dwell,
     Jesus, our Emmanuel.
       Hark! The herald angels . . .

3   Hail! The heaven-born Prince of Peace!
     Hail! The Sun of Righteousness!
     Light and life to all he brings,
     Risen with healing in his wings.
     Mild he lays his glory by,
     Born that man no more may die,
     Born to raise the sons of earth,
     Born to give them second birth.
       Hark! The herald angels . . .

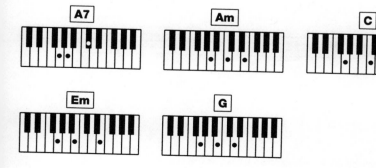

Here We Come A-Wassailing
(Wassail Song)

Traditional

Suggested Registration: Accordian
Rhythm: Shuffle
Tempo: ♩. = 96

Here we come a - was - sail - ing, a - mong the leaves so

green, here we come a - was - sail - ing, so

fair_____ to be seen. *Love and joy_____ come to*

you, and to you, your was - sail too, and God

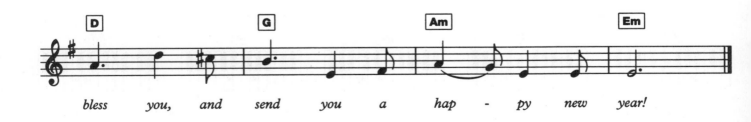

bless you, and send you a hap - py new year!

1 Here we come a-wassailing,
    Among the leaves so green,
    Here we come a-wassailing,
    So fair to be seen.
      Love and joy come to you,
      And to you, your wassail too,
      And God bless you and send you
      A happy new year!

2 Our wassail cup is made
    Of the rosemary tree,
    And so is your beer
    Of the best barley.
      Love and joy . . .

3 We are not daily beggars
    That beg from door to door,
    But we are neighbours' children,
    Whom you have seen before.
      Love and joy . . .

4 Call up the butler of this house,
    Put on his golden ring;
    Let him bring us up a glass of beer,
    And better we shall sing.
      Love and joy . . .

5 We have got a little purse
    Of stretching leather skin;
    We want a little of your money,
    To line it well within.
      Love and joy . . .

6 Bring us out a table,
    And spread it with a cloth;
    Bring us out some mouldy cheese,
    And some of your Christmas loaf.
      Love and joy . . .

7 God bless the master of this house,
    Likewise the mistress too,
    And all the little children,
    That round the table go.
      Love and joy . . .

8 Good master and good mistress,
    While you're sitting by the fire,
    Pray think of us poor children,
    Who are wandering in the mire.
      Love and joy . . .

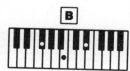

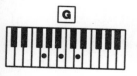

The Holly And The Ivy

Traditional

Suggested Registration: Cello
Rhythm: Waltz
Tempo: ♩ = 112

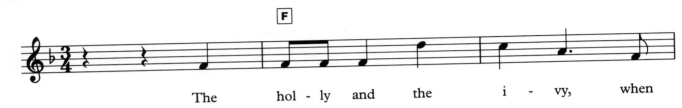

The hol - ly and the i - vy, when

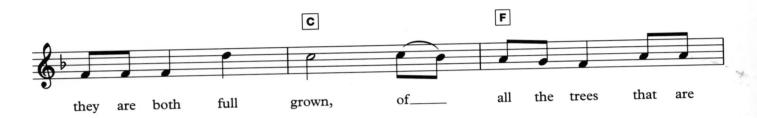

they are both full grown, of____ all the trees that are

in the wood, the____ hol - ly bears the crown. _The_

_ris - ing of the sun,____ and the run - ning of the_

_deer, the____ play - ing of the mer - ry or - gan, sweet_

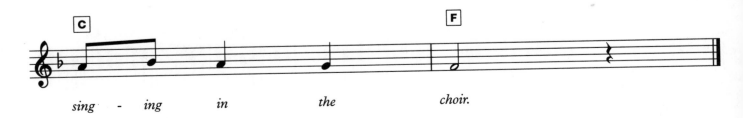

sing - ing in the choir.

1 The holly and the ivy,
When they are both full grown,
Of all the trees that are in the wood,
The holly bears the crown.
The rising of the sun,
And the running of the deer,
The playing of the merry organ,
Sweet singing in the choir.

2 The holly bears a blossom,
As white as lily flower;
And Mary bore sweet Jesus Christ,
To be our sweet Saviour.
The rising . . .

3 The holly bears a berry,
As red as any blood,
And Mary bore sweet Jesus Christ,
To do poor sinners good.
The rising . . .

4 The holly bears a prickle
As sharp as any thorn,
And Mary bore sweet Jesus Christ,
On Christmas Day in the morn.
The rising . . .

5 The holly bears a bark,
As bitter as any gall;
And Mary bore sweet Jesus Christ,
For to redeem us all.
The rising . . .

6 The holly and the ivy,
When they are both full grown,
Of all the trees that are in the wood,
The holly bears the crown.
The rising . . .

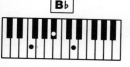
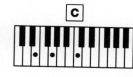
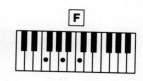

How Far Is It To Bethlehem?

Traditional

Suggested Registration: Flute
Rhythm: Waltz
Tempo: ♩ = 108

1   How far is it to Bethlehem?
     Not very far.
     Shall we find a stable room
     Lit by a star?

2   Can we see the little child?
     Is he within?
     If we lift the wooden latch,
     May we go in?

3   May we stroke the creatures there,
     Ox, ass or sheep?
     May we peep like them,
     And see Jesus asleep?

4   If we touch his tiny hand,
     Will he awake?
     Will he know we've come so far
     Just for his sake?

5   Great kings have precious gifts,
     And we have naught,
     Little smiles and little tears,
     Are all we brought.

6   For all weary children,
     Mary must weep,
     Here on this bed of straw,
     Sleep, children, sleep.

7   God in his mother's arms,
     Babes in the byre,
     Sleep, as they sleep who find
     Their heart's desire.

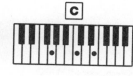
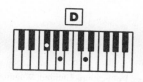

I Saw Three Ships

Traditional

Suggested Registration: Flute
Rhythm: Shuffle
Tempo: ♩. = 92

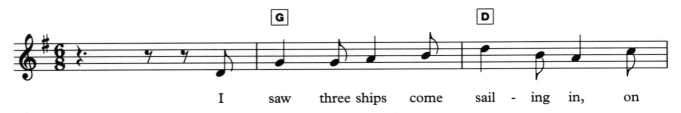

I saw three ships come sail - ing in, on

Christ - mas Day, on Christ - mas Day, I saw three ships come

sail - ing in, on Christ - mas Day in the morn - ing.

1   I saw three ships come sailing in,
     On Christmas Day, on Christmas Day,
     I saw three ships come sailing in,
     On Christmas Day in the morning.

2   And what was in those ships all three?

3   Our Saviour Christ and his lady.

4   Pray, whither sailed those ships all three?

5   O, they sailed into Bethlehem.

6   And all the bells on earth shall ring.

7   And all the angels in heaven shall sing.

8   And all the souls on earth shall sing.

9   Then let us all rejoice amain!

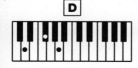
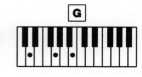

It Came Upon The Midnight Clear

Words by Edmund H Sears / Music traditional

Suggested Registration: French Horn
Rhythm: Soft Rock
Tempo: ♩ = 112

1 It came upon the midnight clear,
That glorious song of old,
From angels, bending near the earth
To touch their harps of gold:
'Peace on the earth, goodwill to men
From heaven's all-gracious King!'
The world in solemn stillness lay
To hear the angels sing.

2 Still through the cloven skies they come,
With peaceful wings unfurled,
And still their heavenly music floats
O'er all the weary world:
Above its sad and lowly plains
They bend on hovering wing,
And ever o'er its Babel sounds
The blessèd angels sing.

3 Yet with the woes of sin and strife
The world has suffered long:
Beneath the angels' strain have rolled
Two thousand years of wrong,
And man, at war with man, hears not
The love-song which they bring:
O hush the noise, ye men of strife,
And hear the angels sing!

4 And ye, beneath life's crushing load,
Whose forms are bending low,
Who toil along the climbing way
With painful steps and slow,
Look now! For glad and golden hours
Come swiftly on the wing;
O rest beside the weary road,
And hear the angels sing!

5 For lo! The days are hastening on,
By prophet-bards foretold,
When, with the ever-circling years,
Comes round the Age of Gold,
When peace shall over all the earth
Its ancient splendours fling,
And the whole world give back the song
Which now the angels sing.

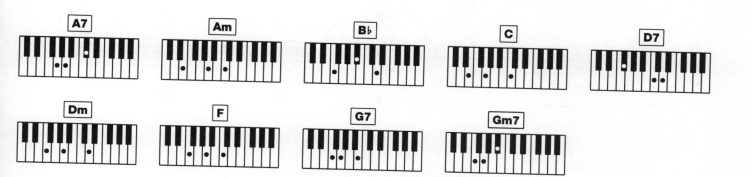

JOY TO THE WORLD

Words by Isaac Watts / Music by Rev William Holford

Suggested Registration: Strings
Rhythm: Soft Rock / March
Tempo: ♩ = 92

Joy to the world! The Lord is come: let

earth re - ceive her King!_____ Let

ev - ery__ heart__ pre - pare__ him__

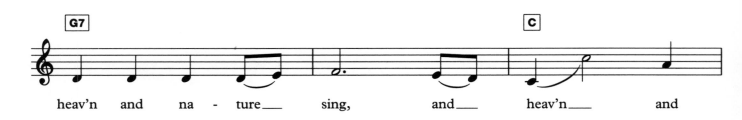

room,_____ and heav'n and na - ture__ sing, and__

heav'n and na - ture__ sing, and__ heav'n__ and

heav'n_____ and na - ture sing!

1   Joy to the world! The Lord is come:
    Let earth receive her King!
    Let every heart prepare him room,
    And heaven and nature sing!

2   Joy to the earth! The Saviour reigns:
    Let men their songs employ,
    While fields and floods, rocks, hills and plains
    Repeat the sounding joy.

3   No more let sins and sorrows grow,
    Nor thorns infest the ground:
    He comes to make his blessings flow
    Far as the curse is found.

4   He rules the world with truth and grace,
    And makes the nations prove
    The glories of his righteousness,
    And wonders of his love.

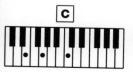

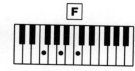

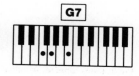

O Little Town Of Bethlehem

Words by Phillips Brooks / Music traditional

Suggested Registration: Flute
Rhythm: Soft Rock
Tempo: ♩ = 100

1 O little town of Bethlehem,
   How still we see thee lie!
   Above thy deep and dreamless sleep,
   The silent stars go by.
   Yet in thy dark streets shineth
   The everlasting Light:
   The hopes and fears of all the years
   Are met in thee tonight.

2 O morning stars together
   Proclaim the holy Birth!
   And praises sing to God the King,
   And peace to men on earth;
   For Christ is born of Mary,
   And, gathered all above,
   While mortals sleep, the angels keep
   Their watch of wondering love.

3 How silently, how silently
   The wondrous gift is given!
   So God imparts to human hearts
   The blessings of his heaven.
   No ear may hear his coming,
   But, in this world of sin,
   Where meek souls will receive him, still
   The dear Christ enters in.

4 Where children pure and happy
   Pray to the blessèd Child;
   Where misery cries out to thee,
   Son of the mother mild;
   Where Charity stands watching
   And Faith holds wide the door,
   The dark night wakes, the glory breaks,
   And Christmas comes once more.

5 O holy Child of Bethlehem,
   Descend to us we pray;
   Cast out our sin, and enter in:
   Be born in us today!
   We hear the Christmas angels
   The great glad tidings tell;
   O come to us, abide with us,
   Our Lord Emmanuel!

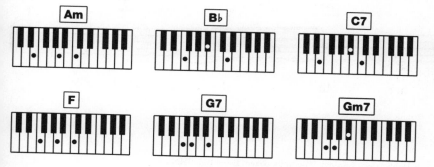

Once In Royal David's City

Words by Mrs Cecil Frances Alexander / Music by Henry John Gauntlett

Suggested Registration: Acoustic Guitar
Rhythm: Soft Rock
Tempo: ♩ = 92

Once in roy - al Da - vid's___ ci - ty,

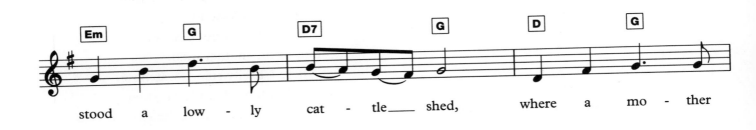

stood a low - ly cat - tle___ shed, where a mo - ther

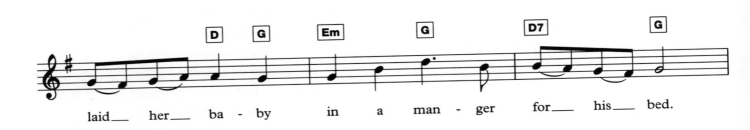

laid___ her___ ba - by in a man - ger for___ his___ bed.

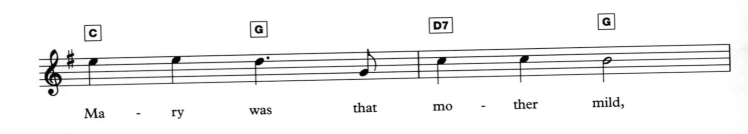

Ma - ry was that mo - ther mild,

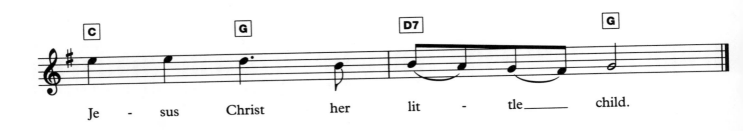

Je - sus Christ her lit - tle___ child.

1   Once in Royal David's city,
     Stood a lowly cattle shed,
     Where a mother laid her baby
     In a manger for his bed.
     Mary was that mother mild,
     Jesus Christ her little child.

2   He came down to earth from heaven,
     Who is God and Lord of all,
     And his shelter was a stable,
     And his cradle was a stall;
     With the poor, and mean, and lowly,
     Lived on earth our Saviour holy.

3   And through all his wondrous childhood,
     He would honour and obey,
     Love and watch the lowly maiden,
     In whose gentle arms he lay;
     Christian children all must be
     Mild, obedient, good as he.

4   For he is our childhood's pattern,
     Day by day like us he grew,
     He was little, weak, and helpless,
     Tears and smiles like us he knew;
     And he feeleth for our sadness,
     And he shareth in our gladness.

5   And our eyes at last shall see him,
     Through his own redeeming love,
     For that Child so dear and gentle,
     Is our Lord in heaven above;
     And he leads his children on
     To the place where he is gone.

6   Not in that poor lowly stable,
     With the oxen standing by,
     We shall see him, but in heaven,
     Set at God's right hand on high;
     When like stars his children crowned
     All in white shall wait around.

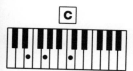
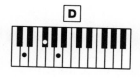

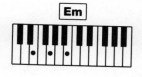
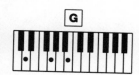

THE ROCKING CAROL

Traditional

Suggested Registration: Vibraphone
Rhythm: Soft Rock
Tempo: ♩ = 104

Lit - tle Je - sus, sweet - ly___ sleep, do not___ stir,

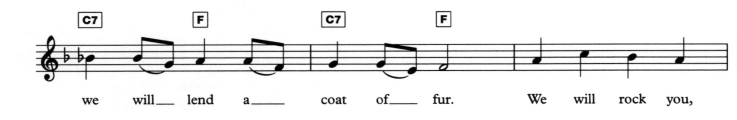

we will___ lend a___ coat of___ fur. We will rock you,

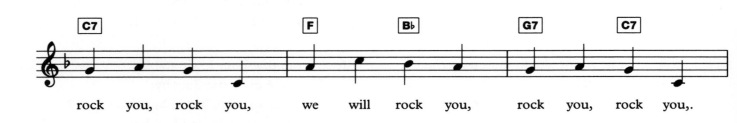

rock you, rock you, we will rock you, rock you, rock you,.

See the fur to keep you___ warm, snug - ly___ round your___

ti - ny___ form.

Ma - ry's lit - tle ba - by,___ sleep, sweet - ly___ sleep,

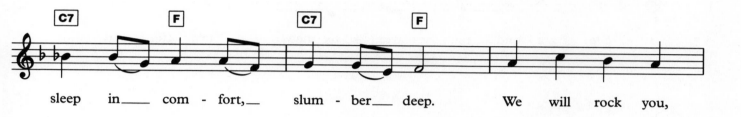

sleep in___ com - fort,___ slum - ber___ deep. We will rock you,

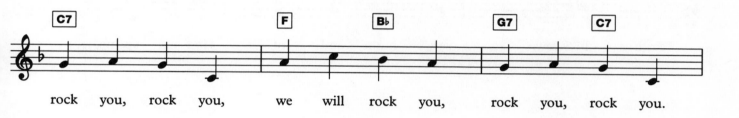

rock you, rock you, we will rock you, rock you, rock you.

We will serve you all we_____ can,

dar - ling,___ dar - ling,___ lit - tle___ man.

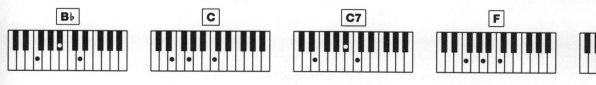

See Amid The Winter Snow

Words by Edward Caswall / Music by John Goss

Suggested Registration: French Horn
Rhythm: Slow Rock
Tempo: ♩ = 92

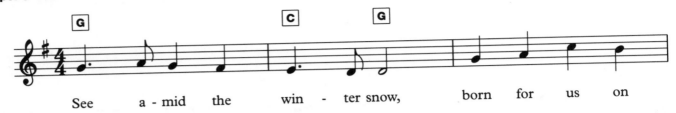

See a-mid the win-ter snow, born for us on

earth be-low, see, the Lamb of God ap-pears,

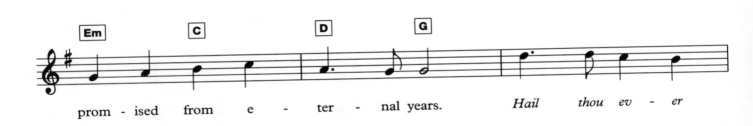

prom-ised from e-ter-nal years. *Hail thou ev-er*

bless-èd morn! Hail, re-demp-tion's hap-py dawn!

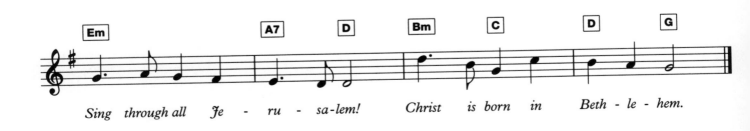

Sing through all Je-ru-sa-lem! Christ is born in Beth-le-hem.

1 See amid the winter snow,
Born for us on earth below,
See, the Lamb of God appears,
Promised from eternal years.
Hail thou ever blessèd morn!
Hail, redemption's happy dawn!
Sing through all Jerusalem!
Christ is born in Bethlehem.

2 Lo, within a manger lies
He who built the starry skies,
He who throned in height sublime,
Sits amid the cherubim.
Hail, thou ever . . .

3 Say, ye holy shepherds, say,
What your joyful news today.
Wherefore have ye left your sheep,
On the lonely mountain steep?
Hail, thou ever . . .

4 As we watched at dead of night,
Lo, we saw a wondrous light,
Angels, singing, 'Peace on earth,'
Told us of our Saviour's birth.
Hail, thou ever . . .

5 Sacred Infant, all divine,
What a tender love was thine,
Thus to come from highest bliss,
Down to such a world as this.
Hail, thou ever . . .

6 Teach, O teach us, holy Child,
By thy face so meek and mild,
Teach us to resemble thee,
In thy sweet humility.
Hail, thou ever . . .

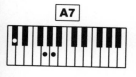 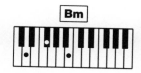 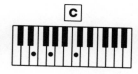 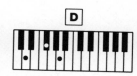 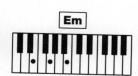

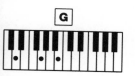

Unto Us A Boy Is Born

Traditional

Suggested Registration: French Horn
Rhythm: Soft Rock
Tempo: ♩ = 132

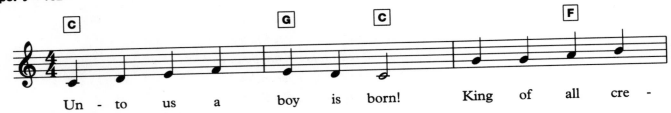

Un - to us a boy is born! King of all cre -

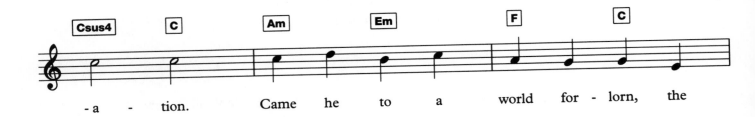

- a - tion. Came he to a world for - lorn, the

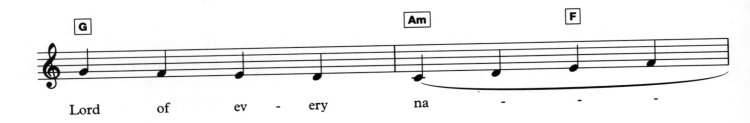

Lord of ev - ery na - - -

- - - - tion.

1   Unto us a boy is born!
     King of all creation.
     Came he to a world forlorn,
     The Lord of every nation.

2   Cradled in a stall was he,
     With sleepy cows and asses;
     But the very beasts could see
     That he all men surpasses.

3   Herod then with fear was filled;
     'A prince,' he said, 'In Jewry!'
     All the little boys he killed
     At Bethl'em in his fury.

4   Now may Mary's son, who came
     So long ago to love us,
     Lead us all with hearts aflame
     Unto the joys above us.

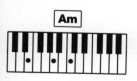 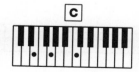  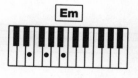 

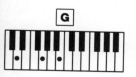

We Three Kings Of Orient Are

Words and Music by John Henry Hopkins

Suggested Registration: Oboe
Rhythm: Waltz
Tempo: ♩ = 160

West - ward lead - ing, still pro - ceed - ing,

guide us to thy per - fect light.

1 We three kings of Orient are,
  Bearing gifts we traverse afar.
  Field and fountain, moor and mountain,
  Following yonder star.
    O star of wonder, star of night,
    Star with royal beauty bright.
    Westward leading, still proceeding,
    Guide us to thy perfect light.

2 Born a King on Bethlehem plain,
  Gold I bring to crown him again.
  King for ever, ceasing never,
  Over us all to reign.
    O star of wonder . . .

3 Frankincense to offer have I,
  Incense owns a Deity nigh:
  Prayer and praising, all men raising,
  Worship him, God most high.
    O star of wonder . . .

4 Myrrh is mine, its bitter perfume,
  Breathes a life of gathering gloom;
  Sorrowing, sighing, bleeding, dying,
  Sealed in the stone-cold tomb.
    O star of wonder . . .

5 Glorious now, behold him arise,
  King and God, and sacrifice!
  Alleluia, alleluia,
  Earth to the heaven replies.
    O star of wonder . . .

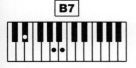
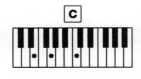
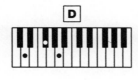
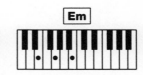
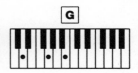

WHILE SHEPHERDS WATCHED

Traditional

Suggested Registration: Piano
Rhythm: Soft Rock
Tempo: ♩ = 96

While shep - herds watched their flocks by night all

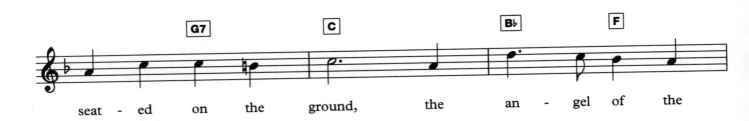

seat - ed on the ground, the an - gel of the

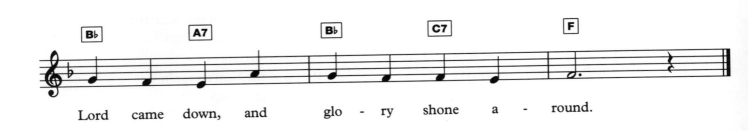

Lord came down, and glo - ry shone a - round.

1 While shepherds watched their flocks by night
All seated on the ground,
The angel of the Lord came down,
And glory shone around.

2 'Fear not,' said he; for mighty dread
Had seized their troubled mind;
'Glad tidings of great joy I bring
To you and all mankind.'

3 'To you in David's town this day
Is born of David's line
A Saviour, who is Christ the Lord;
And this shall be the sign.'

4 'The heavenly Babe you there shall find
To human view displayed,
All meanly wrapped in swathing bands,
And in a manger laid.'

5 Thus spake the seraph, and forthwith
Appeared a shining throng
Of angels praising God, who thus
Addressed their joyful song.

6 'All glory be to God on high,
And to the earth be peace,
Goodwill henceforth from heaven to men
Begin and never cease.'

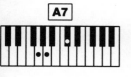
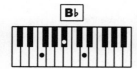
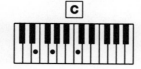
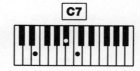
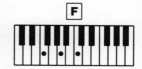

Printed and bound in Great Britain

THE EASY KEYBOARD LIBRARY

THE TWENTIES
including:

Ain't Misbehavin'
Ain't She Sweet?
Baby Face
The Man I Love

My Blue Heaven
Side By Side
Spread A Little Happiness
When You're Smiling

THE THIRTIES
including:

All Of Me
A Fine Romance
I Wanna Be Loved By You
I've Got You Under My Skin

The Lady Is A Tramp
Smoke Gets In Your Eyes
Summertime
Walkin' My Baby Back Home

THE FORTIES
including:

Almost Like Being In Love
Don't Get Around Much Any More
How High The Moon
Let There Be Love

Sentimental Journey
Swinging On A Star
Tenderly
You Make Me Feel So Young

THE FIFTIES
including:

All The Way
Cry Me A River
Dream Lover
High Hopes

Magic Moments
Mister Sandman
A Teenager In Love
Whatever Will Be Will Be

THE SIXTIES
including:

Cabaret
Happy Birthday Sweet Sixteen
I'm A Believer
The Loco-motion

My Kind Of Girl
Needles And Pins
There's A Kind Of Hush
Walk On By

THE SEVENTIES
including:

Chanson D'Amour
Hi Ho Silver Lining
I'm Not In Love
Isn't She Lovely

Save Your Kisses For Me
Take Good Care Of My Baby
We've Only Just Begun
You Light Up My Life

THE EIGHTIES
including:

Anything For You
China In Your Hand
Everytime You Go Away
Golden Brown

I Want To Break Free
Karma Chameleon
Nikita
Take My Breath Away

THE NINETIES
including:

Crocodile Shoes
I Swear
A Million Love Songs
The One And Only

Promise Me
Sacrifice
Think Twice
Would I Lie To You?